GREAT PIANO SOLOS

ISBN 978-1-4234-0304-3

HAL•LEONARD®
CORPORATION
7777 W. BLUEMOUND RD. P.O. BOX 13819 MILWAUKEE, WI 53213

Visit Hal Leonard Online at
www.halleonard.com

CONTENTS

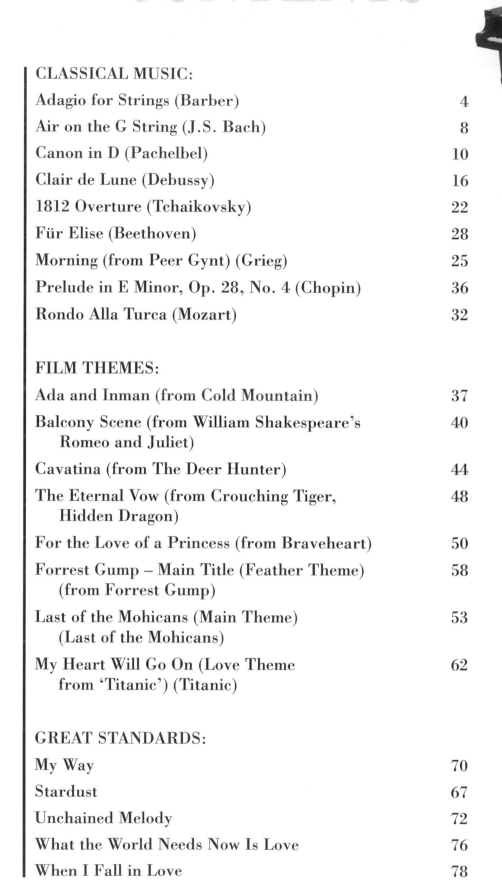

CLASSICAL MUSIC:

Adagio for Strings (Barber)	4
Air on the G String (J.S. Bach)	8
Canon in D (Pachelbel)	10
Clair de Lune (Debussy)	16
1812 Overture (Tchaikovsky)	22
Für Elise (Beethoven)	28
Morning (from Peer Gynt) (Grieg)	25
Prelude in E Minor, Op. 28, No. 4 (Chopin)	36
Rondo Alla Turca (Mozart)	32

FILM THEMES:

Ada and Inman (from Cold Mountain)	37
Balcony Scene (from William Shakespeare's Romeo and Juliet)	40
Cavatina (from The Deer Hunter)	44
The Eternal Vow (from Crouching Tiger, Hidden Dragon)	48
For the Love of a Princess (from Braveheart)	50
Forrest Gump – Main Title (Feather Theme) (from Forrest Gump)	58
Last of the Mohicans (Main Theme) (Last of the Mohicans)	53
My Heart Will Go On (Love Theme from 'Titanic') (Titanic)	62

GREAT STANDARDS:

My Way	70
Stardust	67
Unchained Melody	72
What the World Needs Now Is Love	76
When I Fall in Love	78

JAZZ & BLUES:

Ain't Misbehavin'	81
Bluesette	86
Come Fly with Me	90
Don't Know Why	96
The Entertainer	93
God Bless' the Child	100
Misty	103
Solitude	106

POPULAR SONGS:

Bridge Over Troubled Water	109
Fields of Gold	114
Have I Told You Lately	118
Here, There and Everywhere	128
Yesterday Once More	122
Your Song	124

SHOWTUNES:

Close Every Door (Joseph and the Amazing Technicolor® Dreamcoat)	134
Copacabana (At the Copa) (Copacabana)	131
Do-Re-Mi (The Sound of Music)	138
Hopelessly Devoted to You (Grease)	142
Is You Is, or Is You Ain't (Ma' Baby) (Five Guys Named Moe)	145
Memory (Cats)	150
On My Own (Les Misérables)	155
Till There Was You (The Music Man)	158
Willkommen (Cabaret)	160

ADAGIO FOR STRINGS

from PLATOON

By SAMUEL BARBER

Moderato adagio (very slowly)

(with increasing intensity)

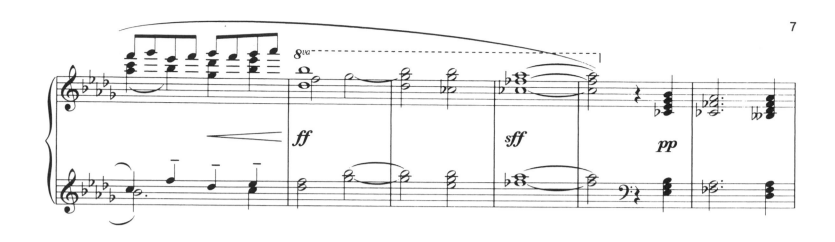

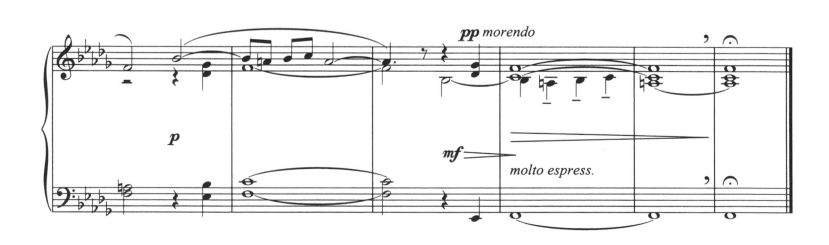

AIR ON THE G STRING

from ORCHESTRAL SUITE NO. 3

By JOHANN SEBASTIAN BACH

Lento, poco rubato (♩ = c.48)

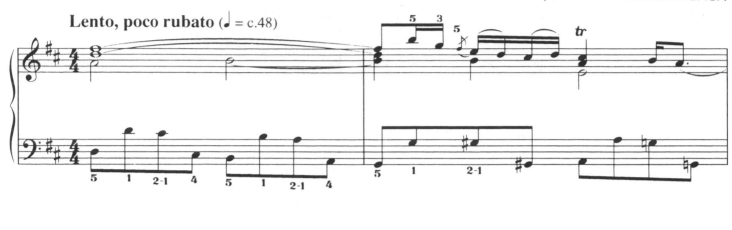

CANON IN D

from ORDINARY PEOPLE

By JOHANN PACHELBEL

Moderato (♩ = 69)

CLAIR DE LUNE

By CLAUDE DEBUSSY

morendo jusqu'à la fin

1812 OVERTURE

By PYOTR IL'YICH TCHAIKOVSKY

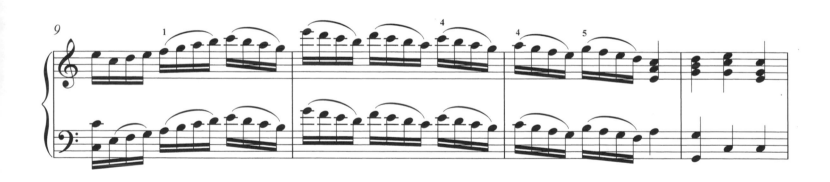

MORNING

from PEER GYNT

By EDVARD GRIEG

Moderately fast

FÜR ELISE

By LUDWIG VAN BEETHOVEN

RONDO ALLA TURCA

from SONATA NO. 16 K. 331

By WOLFGANG AMADEUS MOZART

Allegretto

PRELUDE IN E MINOR, OP. 28, NO. 4

By FRYDERYK CHOPIN

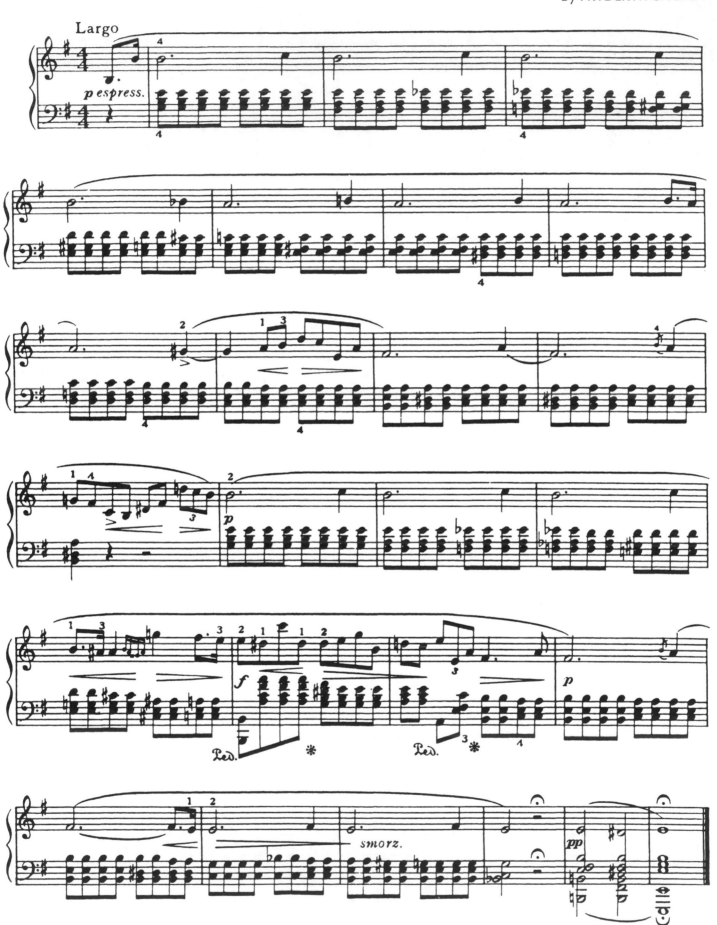

ADA AND INMAN

from COLD MOUNTAIN

By GABRIEL YARED

BALCONY SCENE

from the Twentieth Century Fox Motion Picture
WILLIAM SHAKESPEARE'S ROMEO AND JULIET

Words and Music by NELLEE HOOPER, MARIUS DEVRIES,
CRAIG ARMSTRONG, TIM ATACK and DES'REE WEEKES

CAVATINA

from the Universal Pictures and EMI Films Presentation THE DEER HUNTER

By STANLEY MYERS

THE ETERNAL VOW

from the Motion Picture CROUCHING TIGER, HIDDEN DRAGON

Written and Composed by
TAN DUN

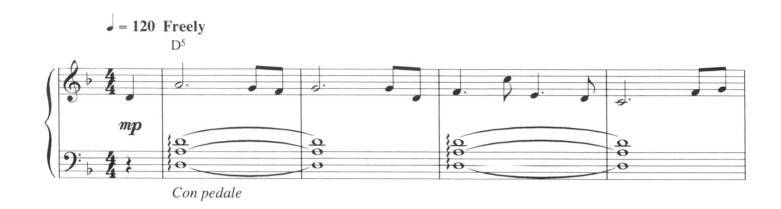

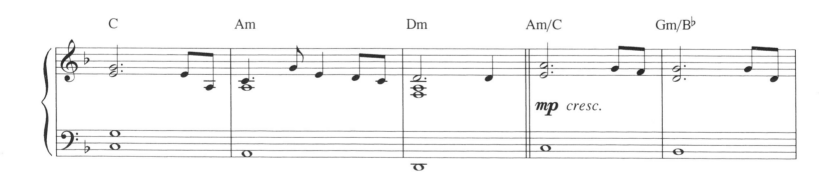

FOR THE LOVE OF A PRINCESS

from the Twentieth Century Fox Motion Picture BRAVEHEART

Music by JAMES HORNER

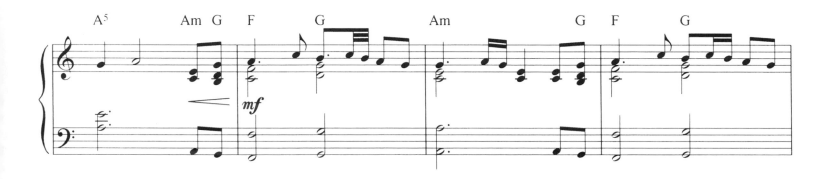

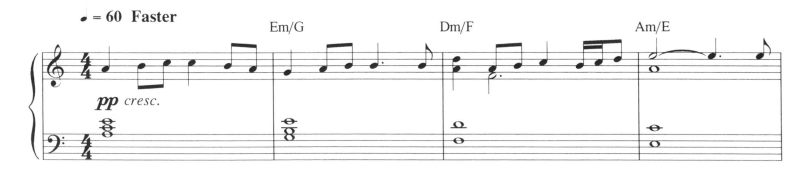

LAST OF THE MOHICANS

(Main Theme)
from the Twentieth Century Fox Motion Picture THE LAST OF THE MOHICANS

By TREVOR JONES

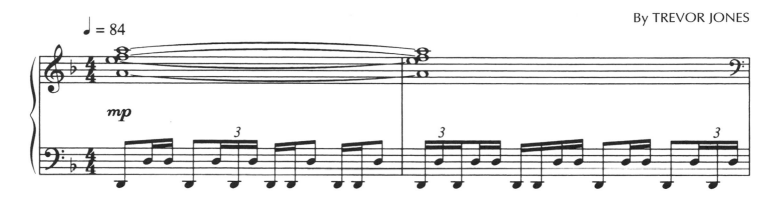

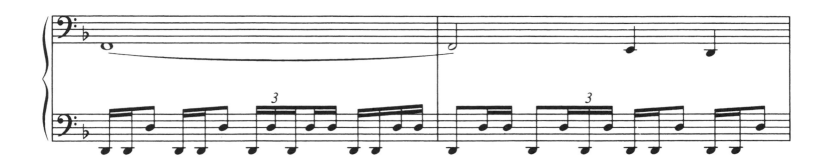

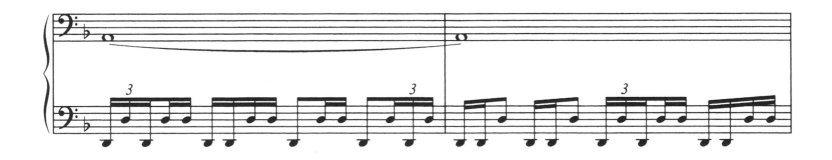

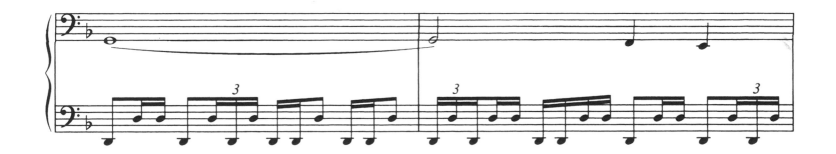

FORREST GUMP - MAIN TITLE

(Feather Theme)
from the Paramount Motion Picture FORREST GUMP

Music by ALAN SILVESTRI

MY HEART WILL GO ON

(Love Theme from 'Titanic')

from the Paramount and Twentieth Century Fox Motion Picture TITANIC

Music by JAMES HORNER
Lyric by WILL JENNINGS

STARDUST

Music by HOAGY CARMICHAEL

CHORUS

MY WAY

English Words by PAUL ANKA
Original French Words by GILLES THIBAULT
Music by JACQUES REVAUX and CLAUDE FRANCOIS

UNCHAINED MELODY

from the Motion Picture UNCHAINED

Lyric by HY ZARET
Music by ALEX NORTH

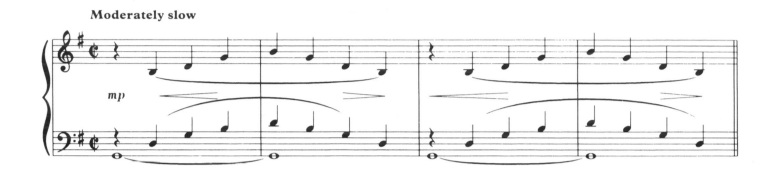

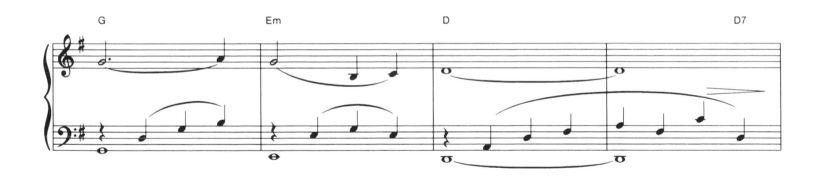

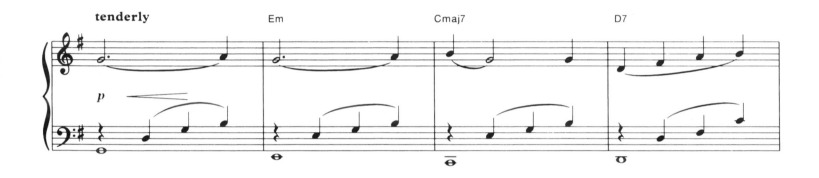

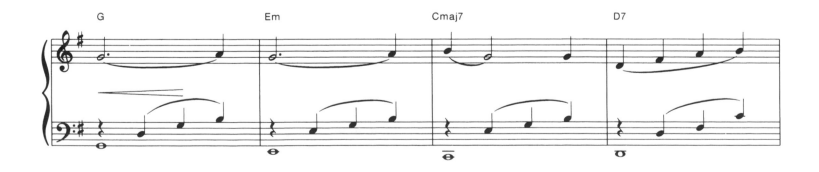

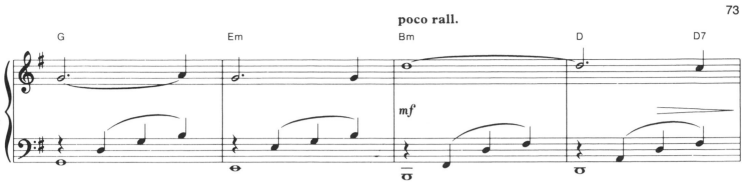

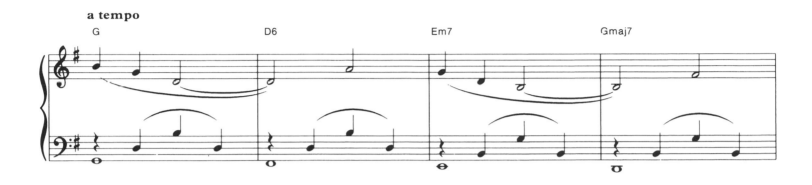

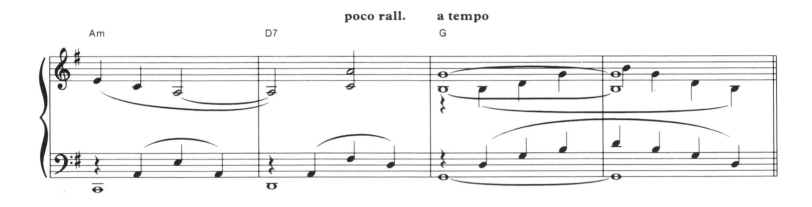

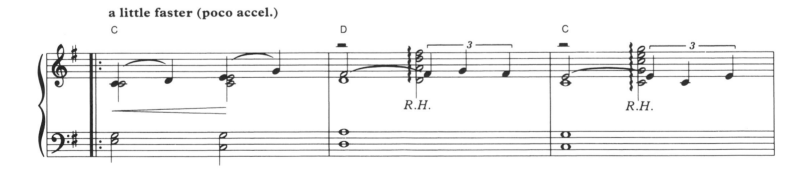

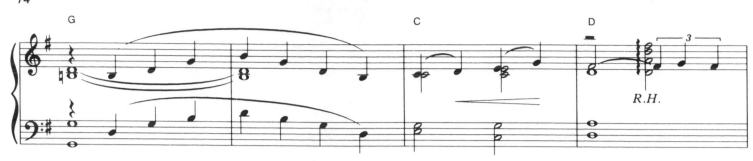

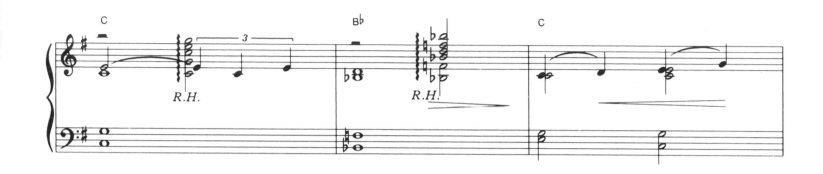

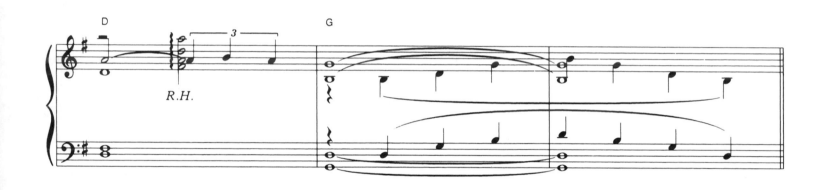

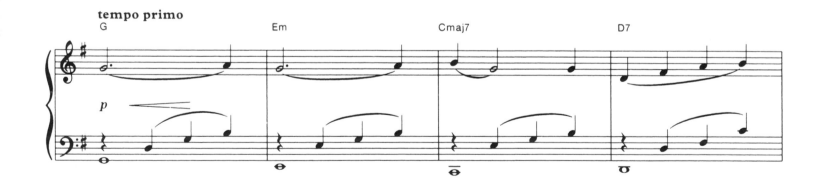

tempo primo

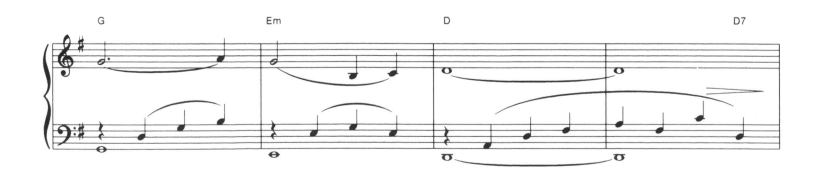

WHAT THE WORLD NEEDS NOW IS LOVE

Lyric by HAL DAVID
Music by BURT BACHARACH

WHEN I FALL IN LOVE

from ONE MINUTE TO ZERO

Words by EDWARD HEYMAN
Music by VICTOR YOUNG

AIN'T MISBEHAVIN'
from AIN'T MISBEHAVIN'

Words by ANDY RAZAF
Music by THOMAS "FATS" WALLER
and HARRY BROOKS

BLUESETTE

Words by NORMAN GIMBEL
Music by JEAN THIELEMANS

Moderately bright

CODA

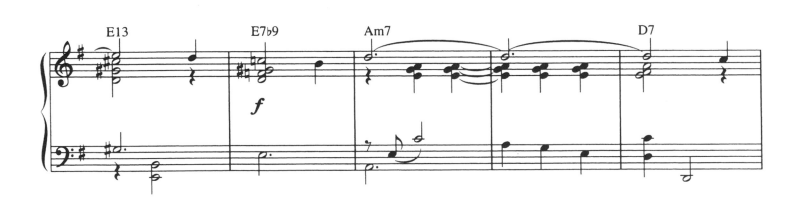

COME FLY WITH ME

Words by SAMMY CAHN
Music by JAMES VAN HEUSEN

THE ENTERTAINER

featured in the Motion Picture THE STING

By SCOTT JOPLIN

DON'T KNOW WHY

Words and Music by
JESSE HARRIS

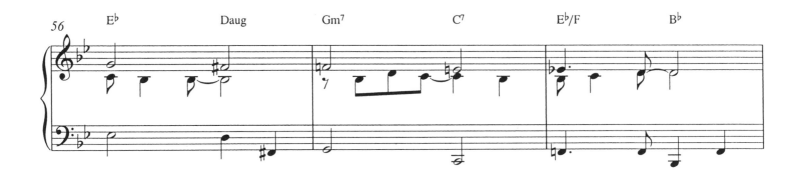

poco rall.

GOD BLESS' THE CHILD

from BUBBLING BROWN SUGAR

Words and Music by ARTHUR HERZOG JR.
and BILLIE HOLIDAY

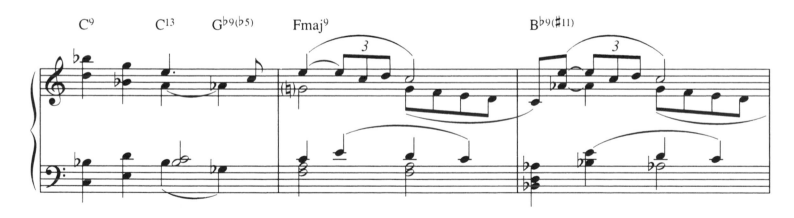

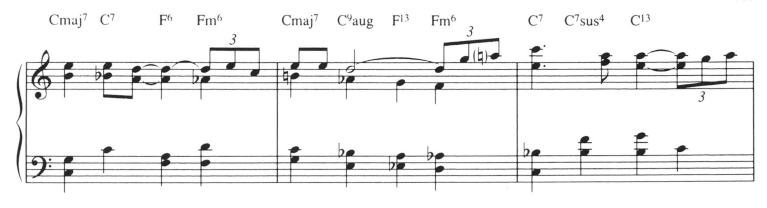

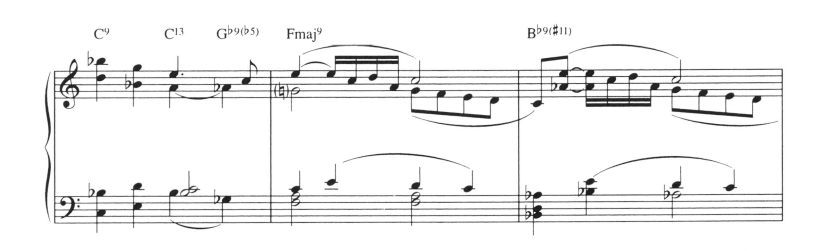

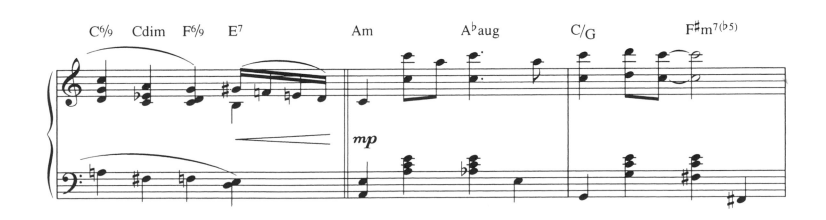

MISTY

Music by ERROLL GARNER

Slowly, with expression

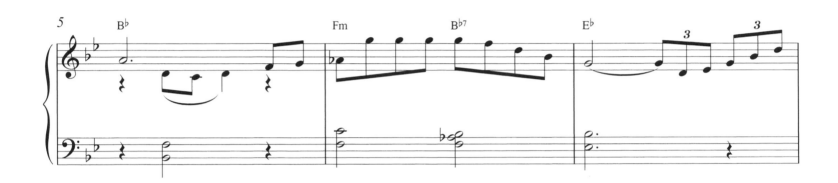

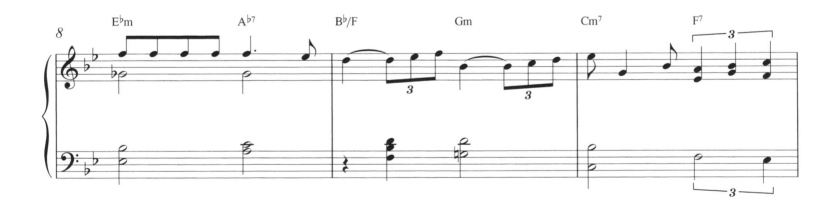

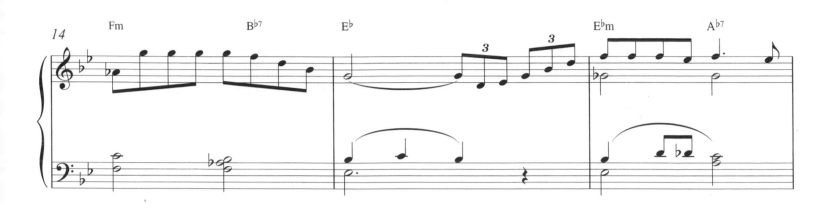

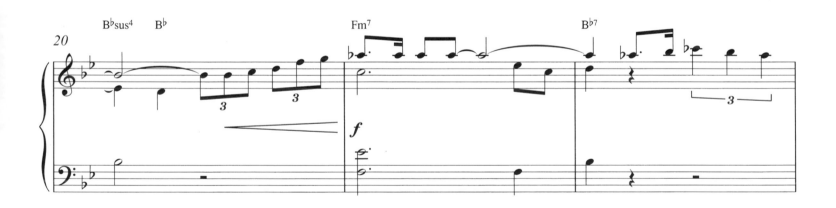

SOLITUDE

Words and Music by DUKE ELLINGTON,
EDDIE De LANGE and IRVING MILLS

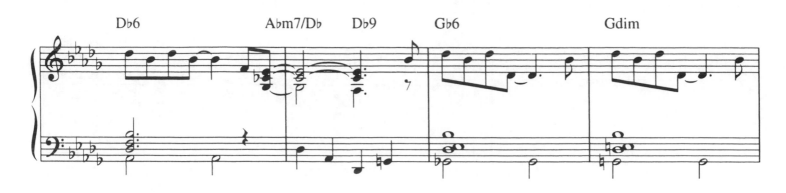

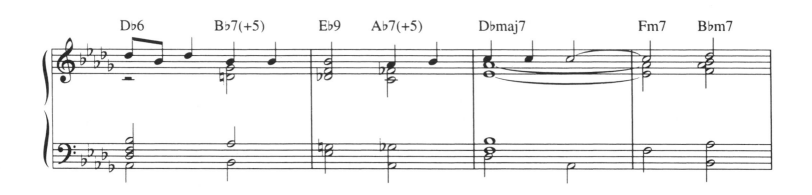

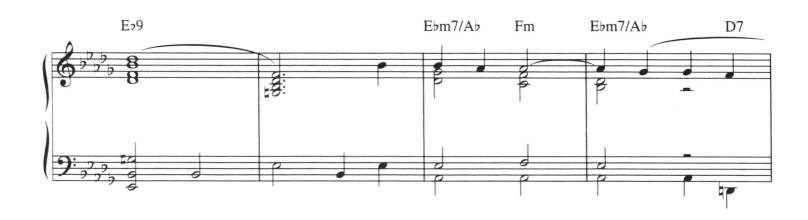

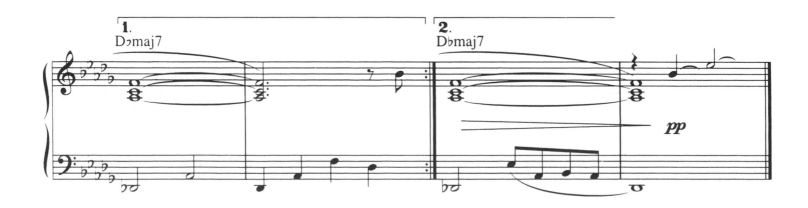

BRIDGE OVER TROUBLED WATER

Words and Music by
PAUL SIMON

FIELDS OF GOLD

Music and Lyrics by
STING

Flowing moderately

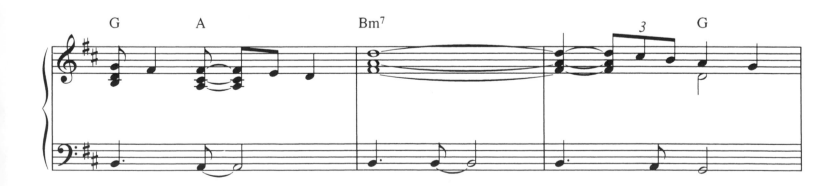

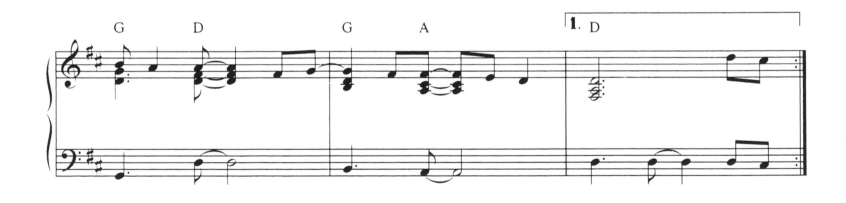

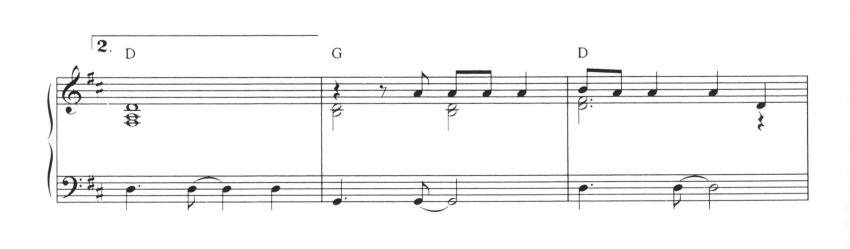

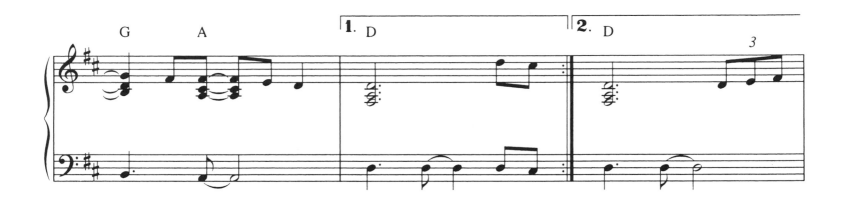

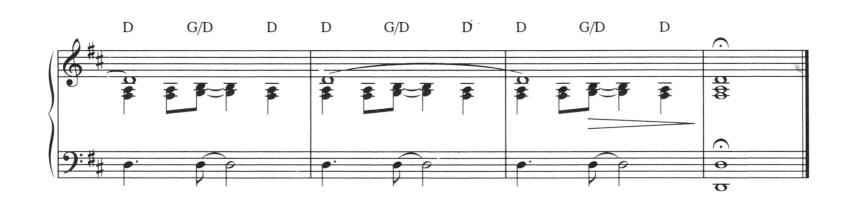

HAVE I TOLD YOU LATELY

Words and Music by
VAN MORRISON

Moderately slow

119

YESTERDAY ONCE MORE

Words and Music by JOHN BETTIS
and RICHARD CARPENTER

YOUR SONG

Words and Music by ELTON JOHN
and BERNIE TAUPIN

Slow, but with a beat

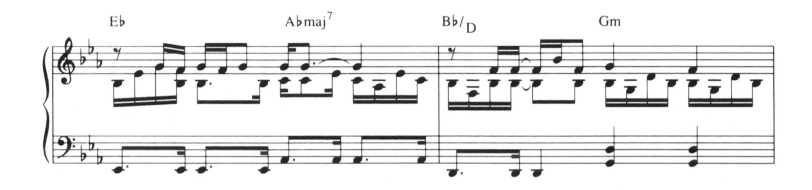

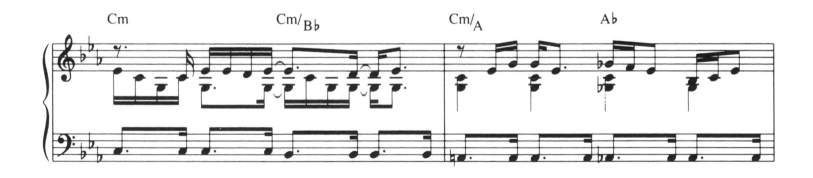

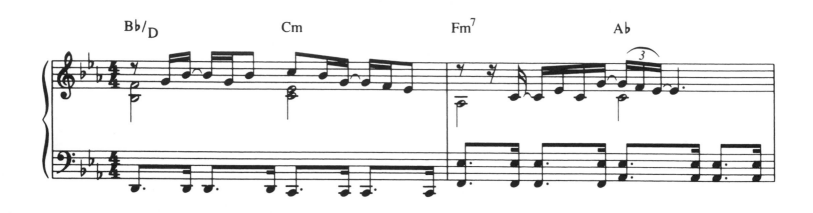

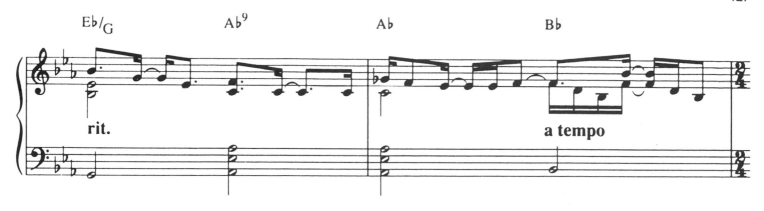

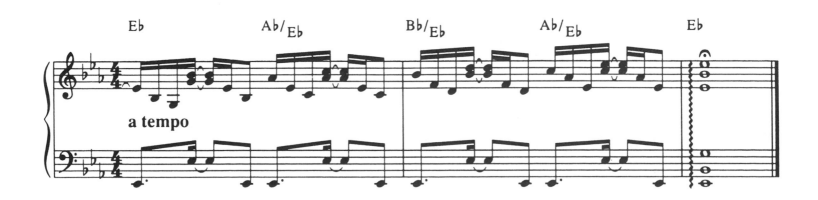

HERE, THERE AND EVERYWHERE

Words and Music by JOHN LENNON
and PAUL McCARTNEY

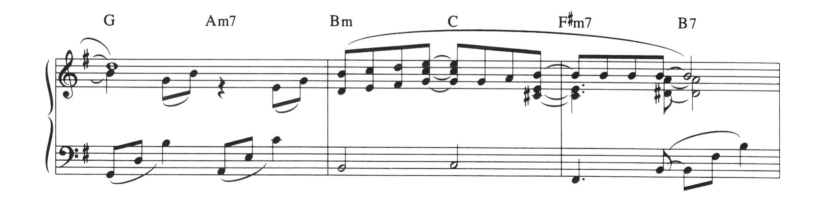

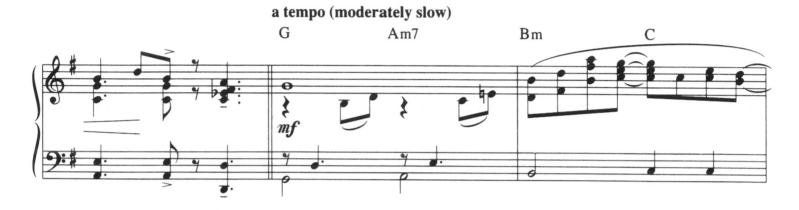

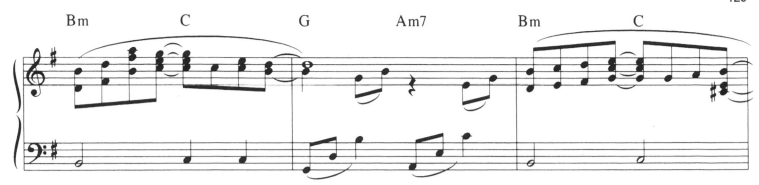

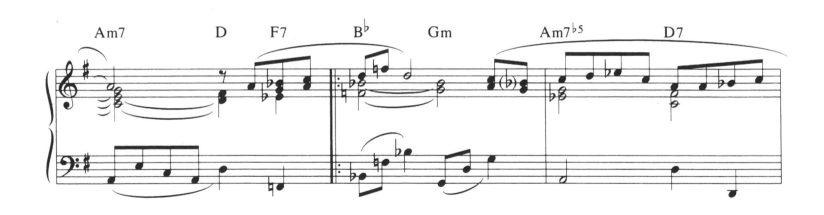

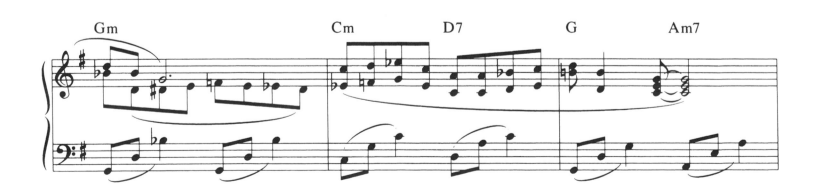

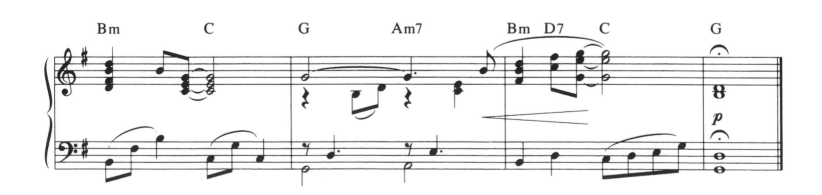

COPACABANA

(At the Copa)
from Barry Manilow's COPACABANA

Music by BARRY MANILOW
Lyric by BRUCE SUSSMAN and JACK FELDMAN

CLOSE EVERY DOOR

from JOSEPH AND THE AMAZING TECHNICOLOR® DREAMCOAT

Music by ANDREW LLOYD WEBBER
Lyrics by TIM RICE

DO-RE-MI

from THE SOUND OF MUSIC

Lyrics by OSCAR HAMMERSTEIN II
Music by RICHARD RODGERS

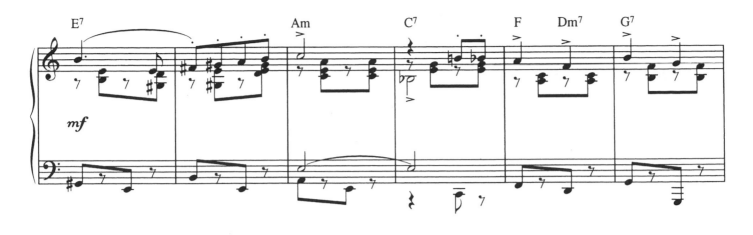

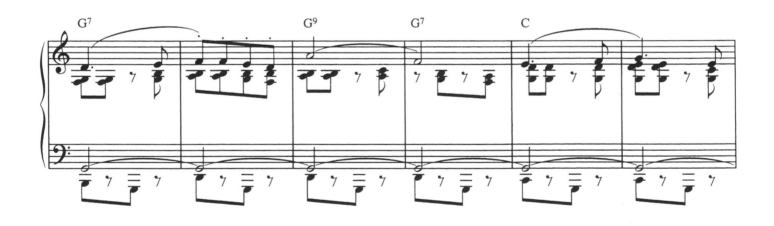

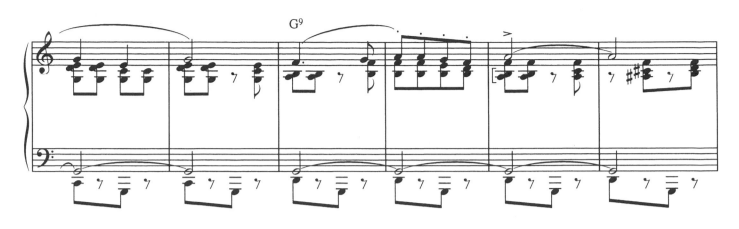

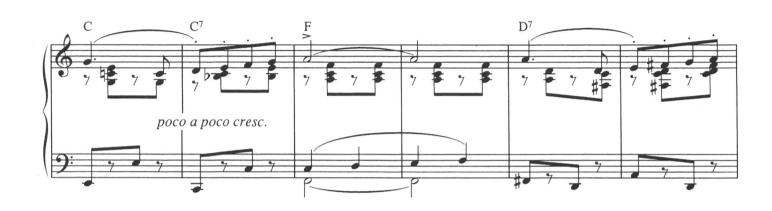

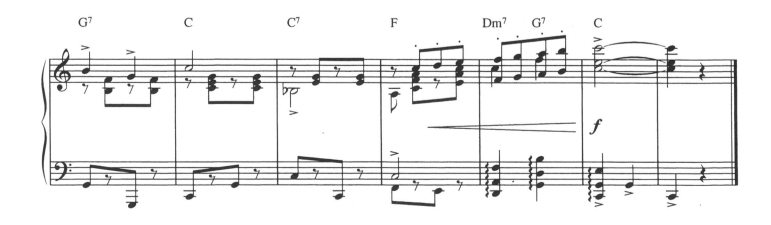

HOPELESSLY DEVOTED TO YOU

from GREASE

Words and Music by
JOHN FARRAR

IS YOU IS, OR IS YOU AIN'T

(Ma' Baby)

Words and Music by BILLY AUSTIN
and LOUIS JORDAN

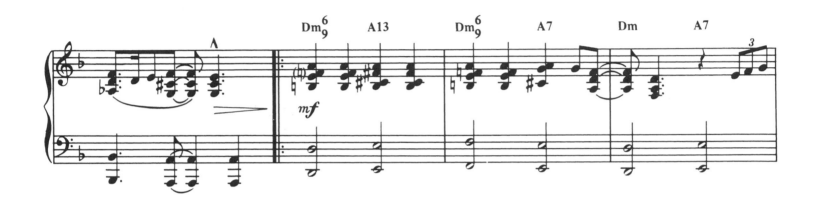

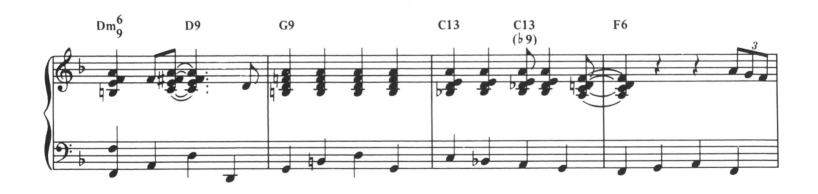

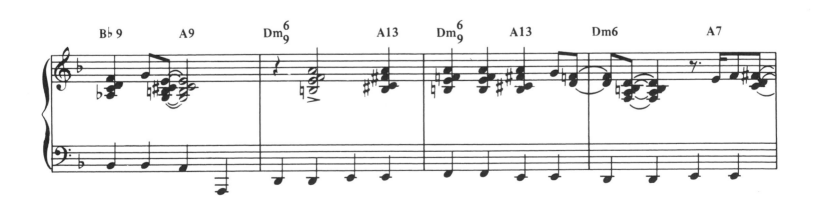

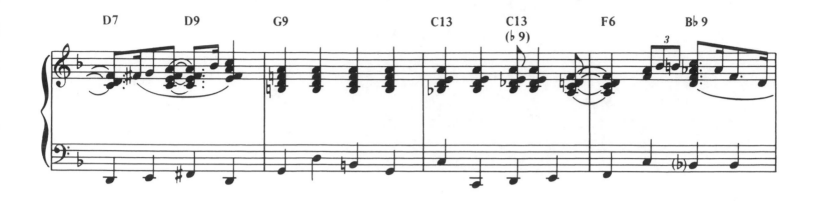

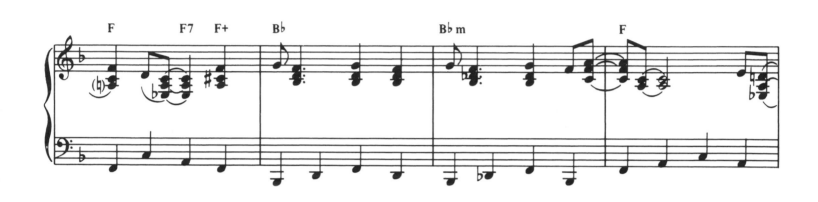

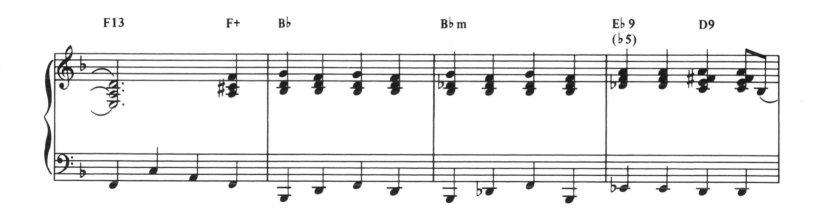

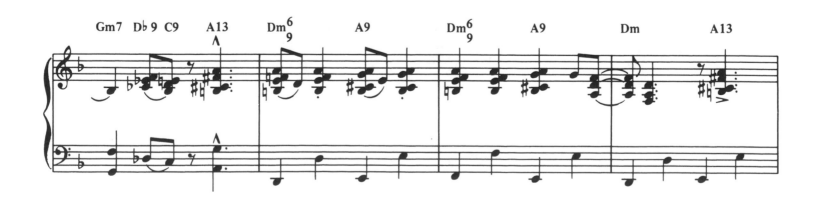

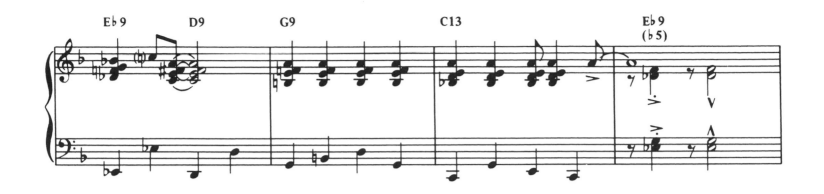

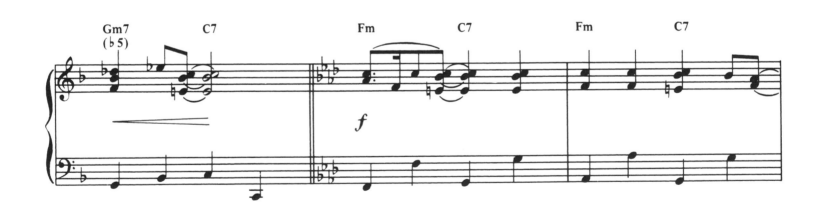

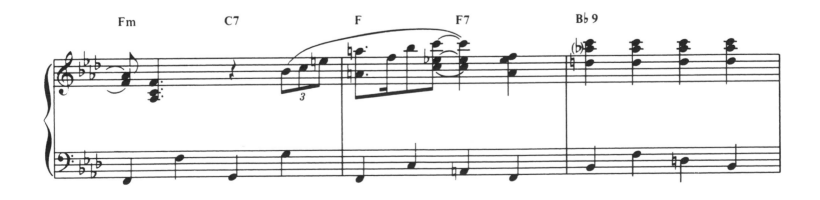

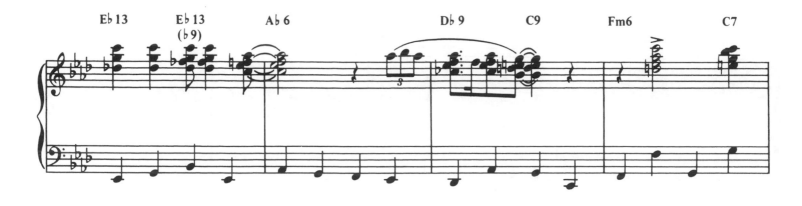

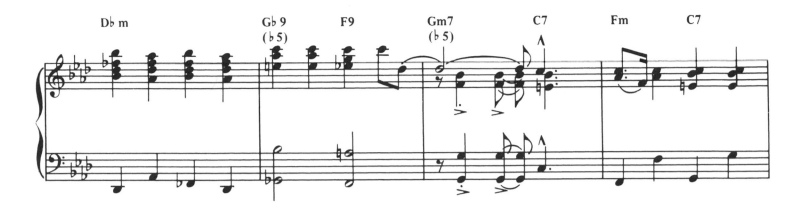

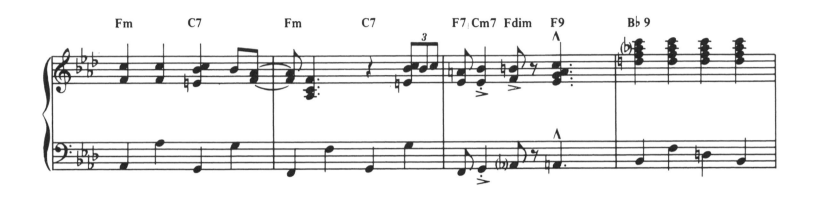

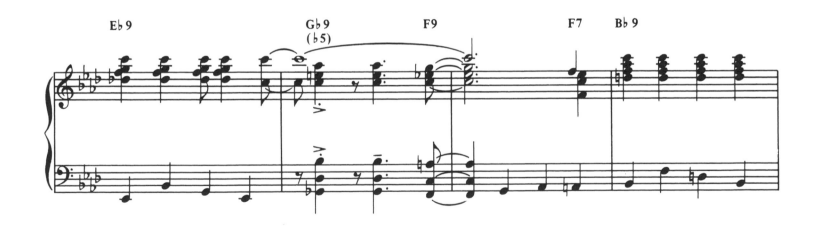

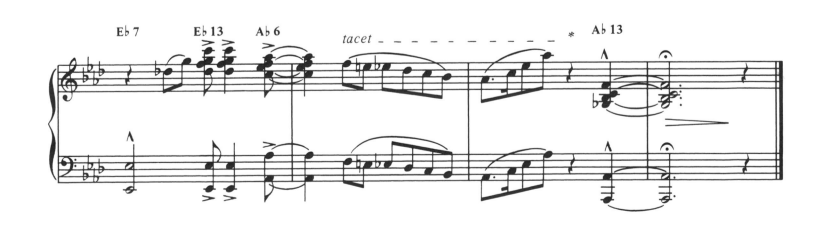

MEMORY

from CATS

Music by ANDREW LLOYD WEBBER
Text by TREVOR NUNN after T.S. ELIOT

ON MY OWN

from LES MISÉRABLES

Music by CLAUDE-MICHEL SCHÖNBERG
Lyrics by ALAIN BOUBLIL, JEAN-MARC NATEL,
HERBERT KRETZMER, JOHN CAIRD
and TREVOR NUNN

TILL THERE WAS YOU

from Meredith Willson's THE MUSIC MAN

By MEREDITH WILLSON

WILLKOMMEN
from the Musical CABARET

Words by FRED EBB
Music by JOHN KANDER

YOUR FAVORITE MUSIC
ARRANGED FOR PIANO SOLO

    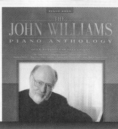 

ARTIST, COMPOSER, TV & MOVIE SONGBOOKS

Adele for Piano Solo
00307585.....................$17.99

The Beatles Piano Solo
00294023.....................$17.99

A Charlie Brown Christmas
00313176.....................$17.99

Paul Cardall – The Hymns Collection
00295925.....................$24.99

Coldplay for Piano Solo
00307637.....................$17.99

Selections from Final Fantasy
00148699.....................$19.99

Alexis Ffrench – The Sheet Music Collection
00345258.....................$19.99

Game of Thrones
00199166.....................$19.99

Hamilton
00354612.....................$19.99

Hillsong Worship Favorites
00303164.....................$14.99

How to Train Your Dragon
00138210.....................$22.99

Elton John Collection
00306040.....................$24.99

La La Land
00283691.....................$14.99

John Legend Collection
00233195.....................$17.99

Les Misérables
00290271.....................$19.99

Little Women
00338470.....................$19.99

Outlander: The Series
00254460.....................$19.99

The Peanuts® Illustrated Songbook
00313178.....................$29.99

Astor Piazzolla – Piano Collection
00285510.....................$19.99

Pirates of the Caribbean – Curse of the Black Pearl
00313256.....................$19.99

Pride & Prejudice
00123854.....................$17.99

Queen
00289784.....................$19.99

John Williams Anthology
00194555.....................$24.99

George Winston Piano Solos
00306822.....................$22.99

     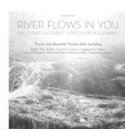

MIXED COLLECTIONS

Beautiful Piano Instrumentals
00149926.....................$16.99

Best Jazz Piano Solos Ever
00312079.....................$24.99

Best Piano Solos Ever
00242928.....................$19.99

Big Book of Classical Music
00310508.....................$24.99

Big Book of Ragtime Piano
00311749.....................$22.99

Christmas Medleys
00350572.....................$16.99

Disney Medleys
00242588.....................$17.99

Disney Piano Solos
00313128.....................$17.99

Favorite Pop Piano Solos
00312523.....................$16.99

Great Piano Solos
00311273.....................$16.99

The Greatest Video Game Music
00201767.....................$19.99

Most Relaxing Songs
00233879.....................$17.99

Movie Themes Budget Book
00289137.....................$14.99

100 of the Most Beautiful Piano Solos Ever
00102787.....................$29.99

100 Movie Songs
00102804.....................$29.99

Peaceful Piano Solos
00286009.....................$17.99

Piano Solos for All Occasions
00310964.....................$24.99

River Flows in You & Other Eloquent Songs
00123854.....................$17.99

Sunday Solos for Piano
00311272.....................$17.99

Top Hits for Piano Solo
00294635.....................$14.99

HAL•LEONARD®
View songlists online and order from your favorite music retailer at
halleonard.com

Prices, content, and availability subject to change without notice.

Disney characters and artwork TM & © 2021 Disney

0422
195

NOTE-FOR-NOTE KEYBOARD TRANSCRIPTIONS

These outstanding collections feature note-for-note transcriptions from the artists who made the songs famous. They're perfect for performers or students who want to play just like their keyboard idols!

ACOUSTIC PIANO BALLADS
16 acoustic piano favorites: Angel • Candle in the Wind • Don't Let the Sun Go Down on Me • Endless Love • Imagine • It's Too Late • Let It Be • Mandy • Ribbon in the Sky • Sailing • She's Got a Way • So Far Away • Tapestry • You Never Give Me Your Money • You've Got a Friend • Your Song.
00690351................$19.95

THE BEATLES KEYBOARD BOOK
23 Beatles favorites, including: All You Need Is Love • Back in the U.S.S.R. • Come Together • Get Back • Good Day Sunshine • Hey Jude • Lady Madonna • Let It Be • Lucy in the Sky with Diamonds • Ob-La-Di, Ob-La-Da • Oh! Darling • Penny Lane • Revolution • We Can Work It Out • With a Little Help from My Friends • and more.
00694827................$24.99

CLASSIC ROCK
35 all-time rock classics: Beth • Bloody Well Right • Changes • Cold as Ice • Come Sail Away • Don't Do Me like That • Hard to Handle • Heaven • Killer Queen • King of Pain • Layla • Light My Fire • Oye Como Va • Piano Man • Takin' Care of Business • Werewolves of London • and more.
00310940................$24.95

COLDPLAY
A dozen of the best from the British band: Amsterdam • Atlas • Clocks • Death and All His Friends • Fix You • For You • Paradise • The Scientist • A Sky Full of Stars • Speed of Sound • Violet Hill • Viva La Vida.
00141590................$19.99

DREAM THEATER – SELECTIONS FROM *THE ASTONISHING*
14 exact transcriptions: Dystopian Overture • The Gift of Music • Lord Nafaryus • Moment of Betrayal • My Last Farewell • Ravenskill • A Tempting Offer • When Your Time Has Come • and more.
00192244................$19.99

JAZZ
24 favorites from Bill Evans, Thelonious Monk, Oscar Peterson, Bud Powell, Art Tatum and more. Includes: Ain't Misbehavin' • April in Paris • Autumn in New York • Body and Soul • Freddie Freeloader • Giant Steps • My Funny Valentine • Satin Doll • Song for My Father • Stella by Starlight • and more.
00310941................$24.95

JAZZ STANDARDS
23 classics by 23 jazz masters, including: Blue Skies • Come Rain or Come Shine • Honeysuckle Rose • I Remember You • A Night in Tunisia • Stormy Weather (Keeps Rainin' All the Time) • Where or When • and more.
00311731................$22.95

THE BILLY JOEL KEYBOARD BOOK
16 mega-hits from the Piano Man himself: Allentown • And So It Goes • Honesty • Just the Way You Are • Movin' Out • My Life • New York State of Mind • Piano Man • Pressure • She's Got a Way • Tell Her About It • and more.
00694828................$22.99

BILLY JOEL FAVORITES
Here are 18 of the very best from Billy: Don't Ask Me Why • The Entertainer • 52nd Street • An Innocent Man • Lullabye (Goodnight, My Angel) • Only the Good Die Young • Say Goodbye to Hollywood • Vienna • and more.
00691060................$24.99

THE ELTON JOHN KEYBOARD BOOK
20 of Elton John's best songs: Bennie and the Jets • Candle in the Wind • Crocodile Rock • Daniel • Don't Let the Sun Go Down on Me • Goodbye Yellow Brick Road • I Guess That's Why They Call It the Blues • Little Jeannie • Rocket Man • Your Song • and more.
00694829................$24.99

ELTON JOHN FAVORITES
Here are Elton's keyboard parts for 20 top songs: Can You Feel the Love Tonight • I'm Still Standing • Indian Sunset • Levon • Madman Across the Water • Pinball Wizard • Sad Songs (Say So Much) • Saturday Night's Alright (For Fighting) • and more.
00691059................$22.99

KEYBOARD INSTRUMENTALS
22 songs transcribed exactly as you remember them, including: Alley Cat • Celestial Soda Pop • Green Onions • The Happy Organ • Last Date • Miami Vice • Outa-Space • Popcorn • Red River Rock • Tubular Bells • and more.
00109769................$19.99

ALICIA KEYS
Authentic piano and vocal transcriptions of 18 of her best-known songs, including: Fallin' • How Come You Don't Call Me • If I Ain't Got You • No One • Prelude to a Kiss • Wild Horses • A Woman's Worth • You Don't Know My Name • and more.
00307096 ....$22.99

THE CAROLE KING KEYBOARD BOOK
16 of King's greatest songs: Beautiful • Been to Canaan • Home Again • I Feel the Earth Move • It's Too Late • Jazzman • (You Make Me Feel) Like a Natural Woman • Nightingale • Smackwater Jack • So Far Away • Sweet Seasons • Tapestry • Way Over Yonder • Where You Lead • Will You Love Me Tomorrow • You've Got a Friend.
00690554................$21.99

JON LORD – KEYBOARDS & ORGAN ANTHOLOGY
14 from the Hammond organ pioneer, including: Burn • Child in Time • Fireball • Here I Go Again • Highway Star • Hush • Lazy • Perfect Strangers • Rubber Monkey • Smoke on the Water • Space Truckin' • Woman from Tokyo • and more.
00125865................$19.99

POP/ROCK
35 songs, including: Africa • Against All Odds • Axel F • Centerfold • Chariots of Fire • Cherish • Don't Let the Sun Go Down on Me • Drops of Jupiter (Tell Me) • Faithfully • It's Too Late • Just the Way You Are • Let It Be • Mandy • Sailing • Sweet Dreams Are Made of This • Walking in Memphis • and more.
00310939................$24.99

QUEEN
13 note-for-note transcriptions from the original recordings, including: Bohemian Rhapsody • Good Old-Fashioned Lover Boy • Killer Queen • Play the Game • Seven Seas of Rhye • Somebody to Love • We Are the Champions • You're My Best Friend • and more.
00141589................$19.99

ROCK HITS
30 smash hits transcribed precisely as they were played. Includes: Baba O'Riley • Bennie and the Jets • Carry On Wayward Son • Dreamer • Eye in the Sky • I Feel the Earth Move • Jump • Layla • Movin' Out (Anthony's Song) • Tempted • What a Fool Believes • You're My Best Friend • and more.
00311914 ....$24.99

ROCK KEYBOARD/ORGAN HITS
29 note-for-note transcriptions for keyboard/organ from the original recordings that made them famous: Born to Be Wild • Dirty Work • Gimme Some Lovin' • Highway Star • In-A-Gadda-Da-Vida • Like a Rolling Stone • and more.
00142488................$24.99

STEVIE WONDER
14 of Stevie's most popular songs: Boogie on Reggae Woman • Hey Love • Higher Ground • I Wish • Isn't She Lovely • Lately • Living for the City • Overjoyed • Ribbon in the Sky • Send One Your Love • Superstition • That Girl • You Are the Sunshine of My Life • You Haven't Done Nothin'.
00306698................$22.99

KEYBOARD STYLE SERIES

THE COMPLETE GUIDE!

These book/audio packs provide focused lessons that contain valuable how-to insight, essential playing tips, and beneficial information for all players. From comping to soloing, comprehensive treatment is given to each subject. The companion audio features many of the examples in the book performed either solo or with a full band.

BEBOP JAZZ PIANO
by John Valerio

This book provides detailed information for bebop and jazz keyboardists on: chords and voicings, harmony and chord progressions, scales and tonality, common melodic figures and patterns, comping, characteristic tunes, the styles of Bud Powell and Thelonious Monk, and more.
00290535 Book/Online Audio $18.99

BEGINNING ROCK KEYBOARD
by Mark Harrison

This comprehensive book/audio package will teach you the basic skills needed to play beginning rock keyboard. From comping to soloing, you'll learn the theory, the tools, and the techniques used by the pros. The accompanying audio demonstrates most of the music examples in the book.
00311922 Book/Online Audio $14.99

BLUES PIANO
by Mark Harrison

With this book/audio pack, you'll learn the theory, the tools, and even the tricks that the pros use to play the blues. Covers: scales and chords; left-hand patterns; walking bass; endings and turnarounds; right-hand techniques; how to solo with blues scales; crossover licks; and more.
00311007 Book/Online Audio $19.99

BOOGIE-WOOGIE PIANO
by Todd Lowry

From learning the basic chord progressions to inventing your own melodic riffs, you'll learn the theory, tools and techniques used by the genre's best practicioners.
00117067 Book/Online Audio $17.99

BRAZILIAN PIANO
by Robert Willey and Alfredo Cardim

Brazilian Piano teaches elements of some of the most appealing Brazilian musical styles: choro, samba, and bossa nova. It starts with rhythmic training to develop the fundamental groove of Brazilian music.
00311469 Book/Online Audio $19.99

CONTEMPORARY JAZZ PIANO
by Mark Harrison

From comping to soloing, you'll learn the theory, the tools, and the techniques used by the pros. The full band tracks on the audio feature the rhythm section on the left channel and the piano on the right channel, so that you can play along with the band.
00311848 Book/Online Audio $18.99

COUNTRY PIANO
by Mark Harrison

Learn the theory, the tools, and the tricks used by the pros to get that authentic country sound. This book/audio pack covers: scales and chords, walkup and walkdown patterns, comping in traditional and modern country, Nashville "fretted piano" techniques and more.
00311052 Book/Online Audio $19.99

GOSPEL PIANO
by Kurt Cowling

Discover the tools you need to play in a variety of authentic gospel styles, through a study of rhythmic devices, grooves, melodic and harmonic techniques, and formal design. The accompanying audio features over 90 tracks, including piano examples as well as the full gospel band.
00311327 Book/Online Adio $17.99

INTRO TO JAZZ PIANO
by Mark Harrison

From comping to soloing, you'll learn the theory, the tools, and the techniques used by the pros. The accompanying audio demonstrates most of the music examples in the book. The full band tracks feature the rhythm section on the left channel and the piano on the right channel, so that you can play along with the band.
00312088 Book/Online Audio $17.99

JAZZ-BLUES PIANO
by Mark Harrison

This comprehensive book will teach you the basic skills needed to play jazz-blues piano. Topics covered include: scales and chords • harmony and voicings • progressions and comping • melodies and soloing • characteristic stylings.
00311243 Book/Online Audio $17.99

JAZZ-ROCK KEYBOARD
by T. Lavitz

Learn what goes into mixing the power and drive of rock music with the artistic elements of jazz improvisation in this comprehensive book and CD package. This instructional tool delves into scales and modes, and how they can be used with various chord progressions to develop the best in soloing chops.
00290536 Book/CD Pack..........................$17.95

LATIN JAZZ PIANO
by John Valerio

This book is divided into three sections. The first covers Afro-Cuban (Afro-Caribbean) jazz, the second section deals with Brazilian influenced jazz – Bossa Nova and Samba, and the third contains lead sheets of the tunes and instructions for the play-along audio.
00311345 Book/Online Audio $17.99

MODERN POP KEYBOARD
by Mark Harrison

From chordal comping to arpeggios and ostinatos, from grand piano to synth pads, you'll learn the theory, the tools, and the techniques used by the pros. The online audio demonstrates most of the music examples in the book.
00146596 Book/Online Audio $17.99

NEW AGE PIANO
by Todd Lowry

From melodic development to chord progressions to left-hand accompaniment patterns, you'll learn the theory, the tools and the techniques used by the pros. The accompanying 96-track CD demonstrates most of the music examples in the book.
00117322 Book/CD Pack..........................$16.99

POST-BOP JAZZ PIANO
by John Valerio

This book/audio pack will teach you the basic skills needed to play post-bop jazz piano. Learn the theory, the tools, and the tricks used by the pros to play in the style of Bill Evans, Thelonious Monk, Herbie Hancock, McCoy Tyner, Chick Corea and others. Topics covered include: chord voicings, scales and tonality, modality, and more.
00311005 Book/Online Audio $17.99

PROGRESSIVE ROCK KEYBOARD
by Dan Maske

You'll learn how soloing techniques, form, rhythmic and metrical devices, harmony, and counterpoint all come together to make this style of rock the unique and exciting genre it is.
00311307 Book/Online Audio $19.99

R&B KEYBOARD
by Mark Harrison

From soul to funk to disco to pop, you'll learn the theory, the tools, and the tricks used by the pros with this book/audio pack. Topics covered include: scales and chords, harmony and voicings, progressions and comping, rhythmic concepts, characteristic stylings, the development of R&B, and more! Includes seven songs.
00310881 Book/Online Audio $19.99

ROCK KEYBOARD
by Scott Miller

Learn to comp or solo in any of your favorite rock styles. Listen to the audio to hear your parts fit in with the total groove of the band. Includes 99 tracks! Covers: classic rock, pop/rock, blues rock, Southern rock, hard rock, progressive rock, alternative rock and heavy metal.
00310823 Book/Online Audio $17.99

ROCK 'N' ROLL PIANO
by Andy Vinter

Take your place alongside Fats Domino, Jerry Lee Lewis, Little Richard, and other legendary players of the '50s and '60s! This book/audio pack covers: left-hand patterns; basic rock 'n' roll progressions; right-hand techniques; straight eighths vs. swing eighths; glisses, crushed notes, rolls, note clusters and more. Includes six complete tunes.
00310912 Book/Online Audio $18.99

SALSA PIANO
by Hector Martignon

From traditional Cuban music to the more modern Puerto Rican and New York styles, you'll learn the all-important rhythmic patterns of salsa and how to apply them to the piano. The book provides historical, geographical and cultural background info, and the 50+-tracks includes piano examples and a full salsa band percussion section.
00311049 Book/Online Audio $19.99

SMOOTH JAZZ PIANO
by Mark Harrison

Learn the skills you need to play smooth jazz piano – the theory, the tools, and the tricks used by the pros. Topics covered include: scales and chords; harmony and voicings; progressions and comping; rhythmic concepts; melodies and soloing; characteristic stylings; discussions on jazz evolution.
00311095 Book/Online Audio $19.99

STRIDE & SWING PIANO
by John Valerio

Learn the styles of the stride and swing piano masters, such as Scott Joplin, Jimmy Yancey, Pete Johnson, Jelly Roll Morton, James P. Johnson, Fats Waller, Teddy Wilson, and Art Tatum. This book/audio pack covers classic ragtime, early blues and boogie woogie, New Orleans jazz and more. Includes 14 songs.
00310882 Book/Online Audio $19.99

WORSHIP PIANO
by Bob Kauflin

From chord inversions to color tones, from rhythmic patterns to the Nashville Numbering System, you'll learn the tools and techniques needed to play piano or keyboard in a modern worship setting.
00311425 Book/Online Audio $17.99

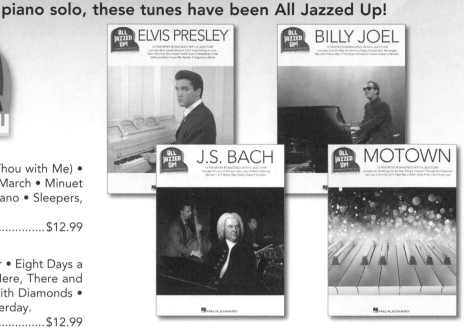

THE ULTIMATE SONGBOOKS

HAL•LEONARD® PIANO PLAY-ALONG

These great songbook/audio packs come with our standard arrangements for piano and voice with guitar chord frames plus audio. The audio includes a full performance of each song, as well as a second track without the piano part so you can play "lead" with the band!

BOOK/CD PACKS

1. **Movie Music** 00311072 .... $14.95
7. **Love Songs** 00311078 .... $14.95
12. **Christmas Favorites** 00311137 .... $15.95
15. **Favorite Standards** 00311146 .... $14.95
27. **Andrew Lloyd Webber Greats** 00311179 .... $14.95
28. **Lennon & McCartney** 00311180 .... $14.95
44. **Frank Sinatra – Popular Hits** 00311277 .... $14.95
71. **George Gershwin** 00102687 .... $24.99
77. **Elton John Favorites** 00311884 .... $14.99
78. **Eric Clapton** 00311885 .... $14.99
81. **Josh Groban** 00311901 .... $14.99
82. **Lionel Richie** 00311902 .... $14.99
86. **Barry Manilow** 00311935 .... $14.99
87. **Patsy Cline** 00311936 .... $14.99
90. **Irish Favorites** 00311969 .... $14.99
92. **Disney Favorites** 00311973 .... $14.99
97. **Great Classical Themes** 00312020 .... $14.99
98. **Christmas Cheer** 00312021 .... $14.99
105. **Bee Gees** 00312055 .... $14.99
106. **Carole King** 00312056 .... $14.99
107. **Bob Dylan** 00312057 .... $16.99
108. **Simon & Garfunkel** 00312058 .... $16.99
114. **Motown** 00312176 .... $14.99
115. **John Denver** 00312249 .... $14.99
123. **Chris Tomlin** 00312563 .... $14.99
125. **Katy Perry** 00109373 .... $14.99

BOOKS/ONLINE AUDIO

5. **Disney** 00311076 .... $14.99
8. **The Piano Guys – Uncharted** 00202549 .... $24.99
9. **The Piano Guys – Christmas Together**
   00259567 .... $24.99
16. **Coldplay** 00316506 .... $17.99
20. **La La Land** 00241591 .... $19.99
24. **Les Misérables** 00311169 .... $14.99
25. **The Sound of Music** 00311175 .... $15.99
30. **Elton John Hits** 00311182 .... $16.99
31. **Carpenters** 00311183 .... $17.99
32. **Adele** 00156222 .... $24.99
33. **Peanuts™** 00311227 .... $17.99
34. **A Charlie Brown Christmas** 00311228 .... $16.99
46. **Wicked** 00311317 .... $17.99
62. **Billy Joel Hits** 00311465 .... $14.99
65. **Casting Crowns** 00311494 .... $14.99
69. **Pirates of the Caribbean** 00311807 .... $17.99
72. **Van Morrison** 00103053 .... $16.99
73. **Mamma Mia! – The Movie** 00311831 .... $17.99
76. **Pride & Prejudice** 00311862 .... $15.99
83. **Phantom of the Opera** 00311903 .... $16.99
113. **Queen** 00312164 .... $16.99
117. **Alicia Keys** 00312306 .... $17.99
126. **Bruno Mars** 00123121 .... $19.99
127. **Star Wars** 00110282 .... $16.99
128 **Frozen** 00126480 .... $16.99
130. **West Side Story** 00130738 .... $14.99
131. **The Piano Guys – Wonders**
   00141503 (Contains backing tracks only) $24.99

7777 W. BLUEMOUND RD. P.O. BOX 13819 MILWAUKEE, WI 53213

Order online from your favorite music retailer at
halleonard.com

Prices, contents and availability subject to change without notice

0322
276